Five Senses

Alan Trussell-Cullen

🔦 Dominie Press, Inc

Publisher: Christine Yuen
Series Editors: Adria F. Klein & Alan Trussell-Cullen
Editors: Bob Rowland & Paige Sanderson
Designers: Gary Hamada & Lois Stanfield

Photo Credits: SuperStock (pages 4, 6, 8, and 10).

Published by:

⌁ Dominie Press, Inc.

1949 Kellogg Avenue
Carlsbad, California 92008 USA

www.dominie.com

ISBN 0-7685-0561-5

Printed in Singapore

13 14 15 16 17 V0ZF 14 13 12 11 10

Table of Contents

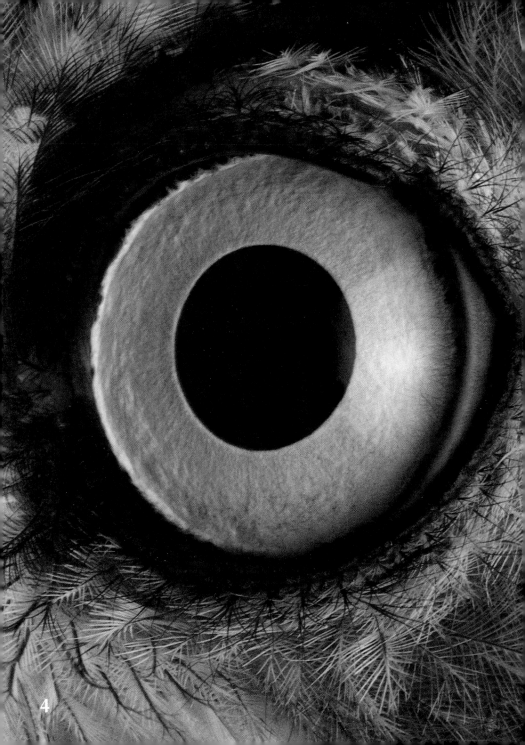

4

I have big eyes.

I hunt at night for things to eat.

Who am I?

I am a horned owl.
My eyes help me see in the dark.

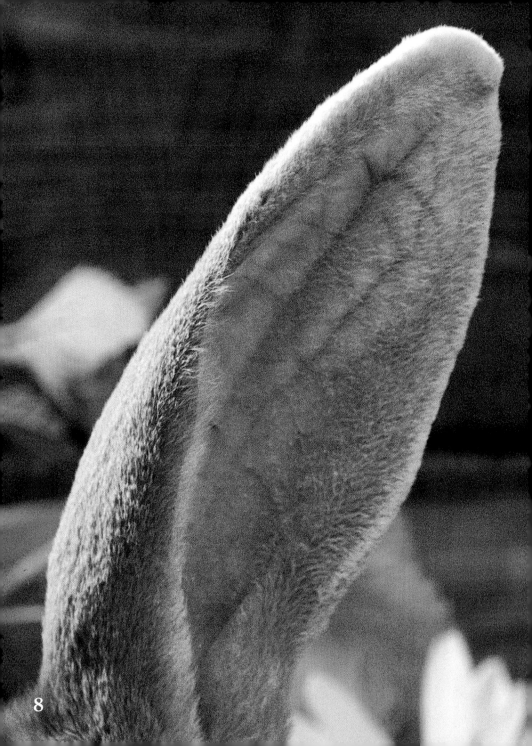

I have big ears.
I listen hard for danger.
Who am I?

I am a rabbit.

My big ears help me hear
when there is danger.

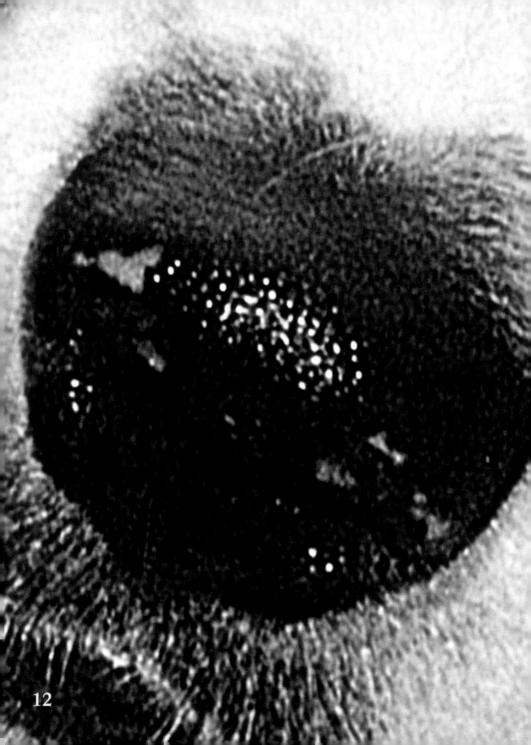

12

I have a special nose.
I sniff the ground wherever I go.
Who am I?

I am a dog.

My nose helps me follow trails.

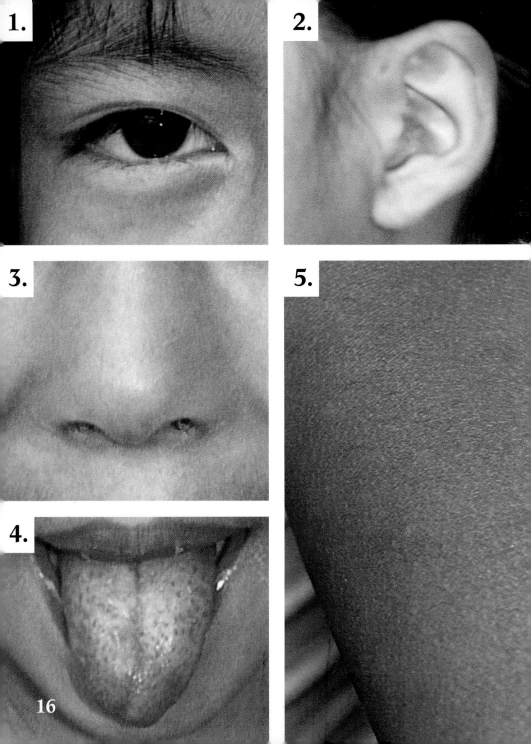

I have eyes to see things.

I have ears to hear things.

I have a nose to smell things.

I have a tongue to taste things.

I have skin to feel things.

Who am I?

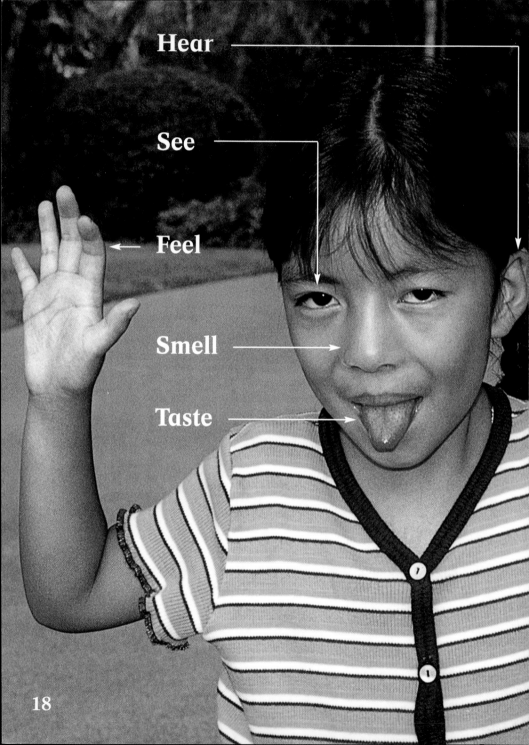

Hear

See

Feel

Smell

Taste

18

I am me!

I am a human being!

Picture Glossary

ear: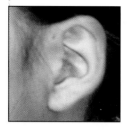

nose:

eye: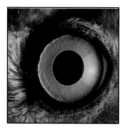

tongue: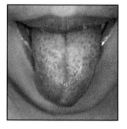

Index